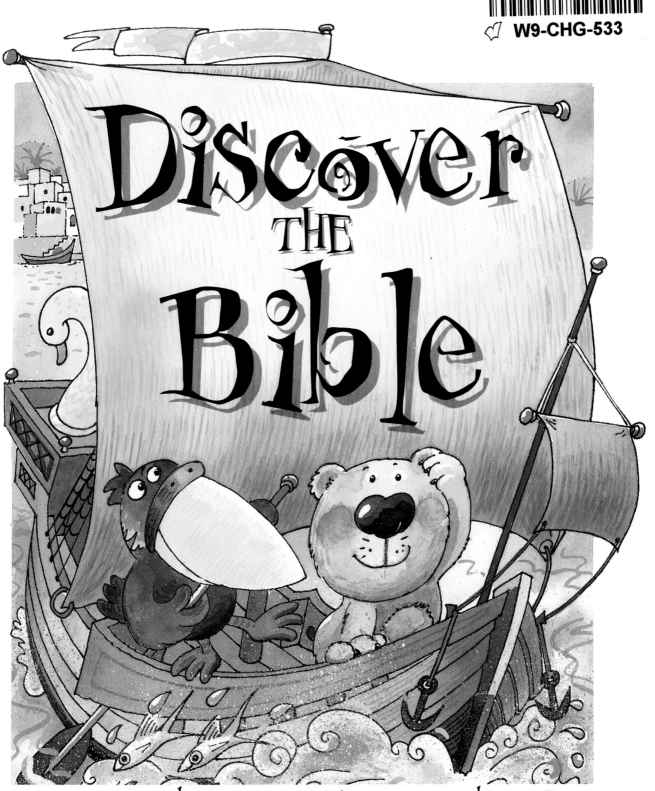

Discover THE Bible

Join the great adventure with Reuben Raven and Hiram Hyrax

Lois Rock

ILLUSTRATIONS BY
Colin Smithson

A LION BOOK

1 What is the Bible?

Have you ever seen a Bible?

A Bible is a big book.

In it are lots of short books, one after the other.

These books were written long ago. Some of the oldest ones were written about 3,000 years ago. The newest ones were written about 2,000 years ago.

And of course, different books were written by different people.

For all that time, many people have thought the books very special. That's because the books aren't *just* about people. They are about people who believed in God, and the stories tell of their adventures with God.

Many people believe they can learn about God too, by reading the Bible.

Most of all, they believe they can get to know God for themselves.

*The old books about the Jewish people are the **Hebrew** Bible and they are still special to the Jewish people. Christians call these books the Old Testament.*

The Bible tells the long story of a people who believed they were special to God: the people of Israel, later called the Jews.

Here are Jews from nearly 2,000 years ago. They have come to their meeting room, the synagogue, to hear their Bible being read aloud.

The teacher, the rabbi, is reading from the old books of the Jews. It is written on a long, long strip of fine leather that is rolled up to keep it tidy: a **scroll**. The words are in Hebrew—the old language of the Jews.

The words being read are from the Bible book called Isaiah. They tell of God's promise to send a special king. Some people think the king has come. They call him **Jesus Christ**. People call them **Christians**.

The writings of the first followers of Jesus are the last part of the Christian Bible today. They are called the New Testament. They were first written in **Greek.**

This is Paul. He believes Jesus is God's special king, the 'Christ'. Paul travels to different places telling people about Jesus. He sometimes writes them letters. Some of his letters are in today's Christian Bible.

Here is a follower of Jesus: a Greek named Luke. He spends time asking people who knew Jesus about the things Jesus said and did. One day, he will write a book about it—and another book about his travels with Paul. These two books, Luke and Acts, are in today's Christian Bible.

2 Telling stories

Some parts of the Bible began as stories told aloud: all kinds of stories.

Some of the stories were about how the world came to be. They helped people think about the answers to important questions:

- Why is there a world?

- Who made it?

- Why is the world sometimes so lovely—and other times so horrible, so hurtful?

After many years, these stories were written down. They include the first stories in the Bible.

The story of the beginning

In the beginning (says one story), God made the world and everything in it. And the world God made was very, very good.

God made people. They were friends with God. They took care of the world. They helped each other.

But people turned away from God, to go their own way. They became selfish and cruel. God's good world was spoiled. People were sad.

The people in this picture are the great, great, ever-so-many great grandparents of the Jewish people today! Day is done—work is over. Grown-ups are telling stories to their children. When the children grow up, they will tell their children…

These two stories are in the first book of the Bible: Genesis.

The story of the flood

People disobeyed God. They became bad. God said: 'I'm sorry I made the world at all. I'll send a flood to wash it all away.'

God saw one good man: Noah. God told Noah to build a boat for his family and at least two each of all the animals in the world.

God kept Noah safe during the flood. Then Noah sent out a dove. It brought back an olive branch. Noah said…

Noah and his family and the animals came out of the boat to fill the world again.

3 The family that grew

The Bible begins with stories about God making the world. The people who told those stories believed God was still looking after the world. God was part of the history of their nation—and that history is in the Old Testament of the Bible.

It begins with a man named Abraham, nearly 4,000 years ago. He was rich, and had a house in a great city named Ur.

But he believed God was telling him to go and find a new home in the land of Canaan. He and his wife would have a child at last, and their son and his wife would have children... as the years went by, there would be more and more people, till the family was a nation.

God promised to take special care of that nation, and through them to do good things for everyone in the whole world.

Here is the family that grew into a nation. The old man is Jacob, a grandson of Abraham. God gave Jacob a new name: Israel. He has twelve sons. You can count them. Their families grew and grew, and became the twelve tribes of Israel.

Jacob's people kept flocks of sheep and goats, which gave them meat and wool and leather.

The story of Joseph

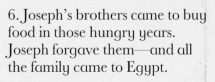

The people lived in tents and moved to wherever there were plants for the animals to eat.

1. Jacob had one son he liked more than the rest: the second youngest, Joseph. Jacob bought him a special gift.

2. Joseph's brothers were angry. Jacob was making Joseph the most important person in the family.

3. One day, they said, 'No more of this. Let's sell Joseph.' They sold him to traders, travelling by camel across the desert with expensive things to sell in Egypt. Joseph was sold as a slave.

4. God looked after Joseph. God helped him tell the meaning of dreams. When the king of Egypt had an odd dream, Joseph explained it.

5. The king gave Joseph the very important job of storing some of the harvest from the seven good years so the country would have food to last through the seven years of bad harvests.

6. Joseph's brothers came to buy food in those hungry years. Joseph forgave them—and all the family came to Egypt.

4 Moses and the great escape

The people of Israel moved to Egypt when Joseph was in charge of the store of food there. At first life was good.

But years passed. Joseph died. Different kings ruled the land.

Four hundred years later, one king of Egypt made all the people of Israel slaves.

They had to make bricks from mud for the king's new buildings.

The people were very unhappy.

A rescuer is born!

The people of Israel grew to hate Egypt. The king ordered that all their baby boys must be thrown in the River Nile to die.

Here are the people of Israel escaping from Egypt. Moses is the leader—but they believe God is the one who has really made the escape happen.

The people left Egypt in a hurry. They didn't even have time to cook all their bread—so they took it with them, in pans wrapped in clothing!

God's laws

As they travelled from Egypt to the new land, God gave Moses **laws** for the people. But two laws said it all.

As they travelled, the people lived in tents. God told Moses to make a special tent: the **tabernacle**.

God made a special **agreement** with the people of Israel: 'I will be your God; you will be my people.'

The king of Egypt let the Israelites go—then sent an army in his best chariots to bring the people back.

The people danced and sang and played tambourines to show how glad they were to be free.

5 A place to call home

Moses led the people of Israel to the edge of a land named Canaan. There, he made a young soldier named Joshua the new leader.

Joshua had a hard job to do: he had to help the people make this new land their home—a place where God's people could follow God's laws and live in peace.

But there were other people already living in the land: Canaanites and Philistines. Some of them liked the idea of living like the people of Israel and following God's laws. Others did not.

The Bible tells many stories of how God helped Joshua and the people of Israel to settle in the new land.

Soon, they were making new homes for themselves and farming the land.

Here is the land where the people of Israel made their home. The walled cities were built by the Canaanites. Outside the walls were the farmlands.

Who should the people obey in the new land? Canaanite gods? Philistine gods? Or the God of Israel—'the Lord'.

As for me and my family we will serve the Lord.

Joshua made his choice.

The battle of Jericho

Jericho was a Canaanite city. Joshua and his men marched round the city every day for a week, as God told him to.

David and the Philistines

People called Philistines lived in the land. They had iron weapons that were stronger than the bronze weapons of the people of Israel. Their soldiers wore frightening helmets with big crests. The Philistines and the people of Israel had many battles.

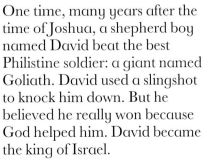

Children helped with looking after the home and the farm. Here, a boy throws stones from a slingshot at wild animals so they don't eat the sheep.

One time, many years after the time of Joshua, a shepherd boy named David beat the best Philistine soldier: a giant named Goliath. David used a slingshot to knock him down. But he believed he really won because God helped him. David became the king of Israel.

He captured a Canaanite city and built a palace there. He called his city Jerusalem. Jerusalem is still the capital of the country called Israel.

6 Solomon builds a temple

King David of Israel won many battles. The nation beat their enemies at last. They soon grew rich. David's son, King Solomon, used some of the money to make David's city of Jerusalem beautiful. He built a palace for himself.

It didn't seem right that the people had fine homes while God had only the kind of tent the people had made when they travelled through the desert. King Solomon decided to build a **temple** instead.

Solomon's temple for God was set on a hill: Mount Zion. He made the city of Jerusalem much bigger than it was when David captured it.
Two bronze pillars stand outside the temple. They have names: Jachin and Boaz.

Inside the temple

The **temple** had one big room. The stone walls were lined with expensive cedar wood carved with flowers, trees, and winged creatures. This was covered with gold. The priest is burning incense on a gold-covered table.

Steps led to an inner room, called the Most Holy Place. In it were two statues of winged creatures, made from olive wood and covered with gold. Their wings reached over the **covenant box**. Only the High Priest ever went in there and saw it—and only once a year.

The temple ceremonies were led by priests. They wore a white tunic, a white turban, and a coloured sash.

Solomon and all the people believed that the temple was just a sign of God being with them. When they looked at the temple, they would remember God and God's laws.

King David had written songs to sing to God: psalms. People wrote many new **psalms** to sing as part of the ceremonies at the temple, to the sound of harps, cymbals, drums, flutes and trumpets.

Here is part of a prayer Solomon said:

God was with our people in days gone by. May the Lord our God be with us now. May God never leave us. May God make us obedient, and help us obey the laws.

7 Hard times

After the time of King Solomon, the people of Israel seemed to get everything wrong.

First, some did not want to obey the next king. They were afraid he was going to treat them cruelly. So the nation split. The part that broke away was in the north. It was called the kingdom of Israel.

The kings and the people there soon forgot to obey God's laws. Some people grew rich and left others poor. Israel became an unhappy place.

After many years, the kingdom was destroyed by enemies: Assyrians, from the lands to the north.

The kingdom in the south was Judah. The Bible says that when they obeyed God, things went well. When they disobeyed God, things went badly.

The Bible says that God kept them safe from the Assyrians. But new enemies came from Babylon. The people of Judah were scared. They did not trust God and what God was saying to them. The Babylonians defeated the people of Judah and took many of them away to Babylon.

The people of Israel squabbled and divided their land in two. Those in the north were beaten by Assyrian enemies, and taken away. Years later, the people of Judah, in the south, were beaten by new enemies and taken away to Babylon.

When the Babylonians captured Jerusalem, they destroyed the temple and took its gold treasures. The precious covenant box was gone—lost for ever.

But they still had God's laws. They set up meeting places— synagogues—to learn about God's laws together.

The fiery furnace

Three young men, Shadrach, Meshach and Abednego, said no to worshipping other gods. They were thrown into a fiery furnace.

The Babylonians worshipped other gods. Some of the people of Judah still obeyed God and would not bow down to the statues.

Prophets

Through all the years, God chose some people to be messengers: **prophets**. They kept reminding the people of Israel and Judah to follow God's laws—to love God and one another.

The prophets also gave the people hope. 'Now the world feels dark and sad,' they said...

8 A boy is born in Bethlehem

The people of Judah were exiles in Babylon for about 60 years. They became known as the **Jews**. Then people called Persians beat the Babylonians. They sent the Jews back home.

It was hard work rebuilding the city of Jerusalem. The new temple was not as grand as the one Solomon had built.

Worse, the people were never really free. After the Persians, the Greeks ruled the land. Later, the Romans were in charge.

The Jews *did* have kings, but they only made sure everyone obeyed the Romans. One king, named Herod, built a splendid new **temple**.

But he did not really love God or other people. He was cruel.

Would God's king ever come?

About 2000 years ago, a baby was born in a little town in Israel called Bethlehem. His name was Jesus. His mother, Mary, had amazing news to tell.

Months before, an angel had told her that she was going to have a baby. And the angel had said the baby would be God's son.

But just look at the room where he is born— it's an animal room! God hasn't come as a rich king.

The special baby

1. Mary, Jesus' mother, had promised to marry a man named Joseph. The Bible says that an angel told him to take care of Mary and her special baby—and that is what he did.

2. Mary and Joseph were only visiting Bethlehem when Jesus was born. All the proper rooms for visitors were full, and Jesus was born in an animal room.

The wise men and the star

One Bible story says that on the night Jesus was born, shepherds were out on the hills near Bethlehem watching their sheep.

3. Jesus was wrapped in strips of cloth called swaddling clothes. All babies were swaddled to keep them feeling safe and snug.

4. Jesus was cradled in a manger—the place where people put food for the animals.

Some time later, wise men in lands to the east saw a star.

They believed it would lead them to a king. But King Herod in Jerusalem didn't know of a new king.

The wise men brought three expensive gifts fit for a king: gold, frankincense and myrrh.

9 Jesus and friends

The Bible doesn't say much about Jesus growing up. Some time after he was born in Bethlehem, Mary and Joseph took him to their home in Nazareth.

It was a town among hills, with little fields cut into the slopes—terraces. Here people grew grain, figs, olives and grapevines.

Jesus learned to do the same work as Joseph: he became a builder and carpenter.

When he was about thirty, he began a new kind of work: telling people about God and about how people could be friends with God.

Jesus made many friends.

The baby Jesus grew up. Some of his best friends were young men who fished on Lake Galilee, a large lake just a day's walk from Nazareth. In the boat are Peter, Andrew, James and John.

So God's king Jesus had to do work like this.

God must know what it is like to feel ordinary.

People often turn away from people who are sick: they are scared they'll get the same illness.

People can be cruel to anyone who is found doing wrong things.

Jesus was a friend to children. Grown-ups could wait when he wanted to spend time with children.

Jesus travelled to many towns around Lake Galilee on his friends' fishing boats, which had big sails to catch the wind and oars for rowing on calm days. The big oars at the back are to steer the boat.

Not many people liked the Romans who ruled the land, but Jesus was kind to them. He showed that Romans were important to God as well as Jews.

God's love and care

Jesus noticed the wild creatures, such as sparrows. He said that God loved them and took care of them and noticed when they got hurt.

In spring the hillsides around Lake Galilee are covered with beautiful flowers. Jesus said that God takes care of the flowers— so just think how much more God takes care of people.

10 Jesus and his stories

When Jesus talked, lots of people came to listen.

He told stories about everyday things: looking after children, children who disobey parents, looking after animals, growing seeds, having a party...

Everything he said helped people understand more about God.

He said that God loves people and forgives them when they get things wrong.

He said that the most important thing for anyone to do is to be God's friend.

Crowds gather to hear Jesus. And they stay for hours!

What is God like?

'God is like someone who is throwing a party,' said Jesus. 'When you get your invitation, you COME. Or you miss out in a big way.'

Jesus said that God is like a kind parent who welcomes back a child, even when they have made a mess of things.

A good shepherd risks all kind of danger to take care of all the sheep, and goes looking for the one sheep in a hundred who gets lost. Jesus said that God goes looking for the person who feels lost and alone and welcomes them as a friend.

A farming story

'One day,' said Jesus, 'a farmer went out to sow seeds—scattering them from a basket onto the field. The seeds fell in different places'.

Some seeds fell on a hard path. Birds gobbled them up.

Some seeds fell in shallow, stony soil. They grew fast... but they wilted in the sun.

Some seeds fell among weeds. They grew, but the weeds were stronger.

Some seeds fell in good soil: they grew a harvest of grain.

Some stories help me see how God loves people.

Others show how I should love God... and other people.

11 Jesus' week in Jerusalem

Jesus had many friends. The people who lived rotten lives and had no friends till they met Jesus liked him best of all!

Some of the people who felt they lived good lives were not so sure. They didn't like all this talk about God forgiving people. How dare Jesus talk about God anyway!

One week, when Jesus came to Jerusalem for a special festival, Jesus' enemies decided it was time to get rid of him.

The day Jesus rode into Jerusalem on a donkey, many people welcomed him as a king. Before the week was over, many had turned against him.

Hooray for Jesus! Hooray for God's king!

Jesus and the last supper

Jesus and his friends met for a special meal. Who was going to be the servant and wash people's dusty feet?

The special meal was called the Passover.

Jesus shared bread and wine as part of the meal.

Some of the people who thought they knew all about God were called Pharisees. They knew God's laws, but some were unloving and unforgiving.

Many Pharisees hated Jesus because he forgave people *and made them well*.

The priests worked in God's temple. They felt they knew all about God. They wanted Jesus and his strange ideas about God right out of the way.

Judas was one of Jesus' close friends.

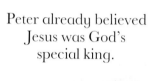

Peter already believed Jesus was God's special king.

Pontius Pilate was the Roman in charge of Jerusalem at that time. He knew Jesus had done no wrong. But the priests and the crowd wanted him dead—so he agreed to have Jesus killed.

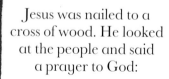

Jesus was nailed to a cross of wood. He looked at the people and said a prayer to God:

Many people loved Jesus as a real friend.

They got pushed out of the way as Jesus was taken away to die.

Roman soldiers made sure Roman laws were obeyed.

They had the job of putting Jesus to death. He was nailed to a cross of wood—crucified.

12 Is Jesus alive?

Jesus died on a cross. Some brave friends asked if they could take the body away. They put it in a stone tomb.

But the weekly day of rest, the sabbath, was beginning. There was no time to do the burial properly. So they rolled the stone door in place and left the body.

Jesus was dead. A rich man, Joseph of Arimathea, put the body in a tomb like a little cave cut into the rock. A big, round stone set in a groove was rolled in front as the door.

People say the tomb was in a garden. Perhaps it was an olive grove.

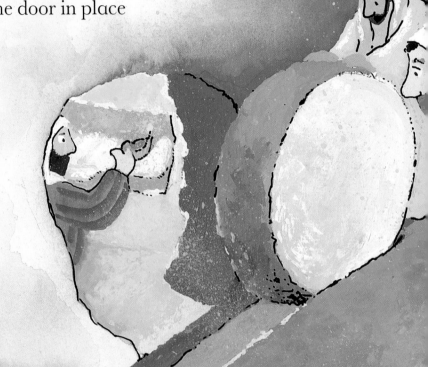

Where is Jesus?

The stone door of Jesus' tomb was shut before the sabbath. It was heavy.

People put the body on a stone ledge, wrapped in bandages.

The first people to come to the tomb after the sabbath said they saw bright, shining figures.

I'm going fishing

Peter had run away when people came to arrest Jesus. Then Jesus had been killed. Peter and some others went home to Galilee. All the good times with Jesus were over. 'I'm going fishing,' said Peter.

They went out. But they caught nothing.

As they came back they saw someone on the shore. He told them where to cast their nets.

Then Peter knew who the man was. 'It's Jesus!'

Jesus' friend Mary Magdalene saw a man nearby. 'Perhaps he's the gardener,' she thought. 'I'll ask him what he knows.'

If God gave Jesus new life, then all the bad things didn't win—God did!

No more need for crying then!

13 Christians

Forty days after Jesus came back to life, he said goodbye to his friends.

'I am going to be with God,' he said. 'Wait a bit. I will come back to you in a special way. You will know when it happens. I will be with you always then as a friend, to help you in all you do.'

Ten days later came a festival called Pentecost. Jesus' followers saw something like flames above their heads. They heard a noise like a strong wind. And they felt a special kind of happiness inside—Jesus with them!

Bravely they went out to tell everyone their good news: Jesus had risen from the dead. God is never beaten, not even when people do their worst. Death isn't the end.

Jesus was God's special king: God in person, come to make a way back to God, so everyone could be God's friends for ever. And they could know Jesus was with them, too.

Many people believed this good news. Soon, they were meeting together: the first **Christians**, and the first **churches**. The good news about Jesus wasn't just for Jews. Greeks, Romans— everyone was welcome. The promise made to Abraham had come true: God had done good things for everyone in the world, all through Abraham's family.

The first followers of Jesus met in each other's homes. This meeting is in a home of Jesus' day: a Roman villa. Everyone was welcome. Now they were all God's family together.

Some Christians travelled, spreading the news.

People who wanted to follow Jesus were baptized: dipped in water, to show they were making a new start as God's friends.

Christians shared meals together. When they shared bread and wine, they remembered Jesus' last supper with his friends, and God's new agreement with people.

People brought their friends along to meet with other Christians. Everyone was welcome.

The good news about Jesus has been spreading ever since. People can read it in the second part of the Bible—the New Testament.

Millions of people today read it. And many of them decide to follow Jesus, too.

Index

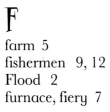

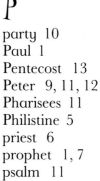
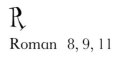